OPEN WIDE!

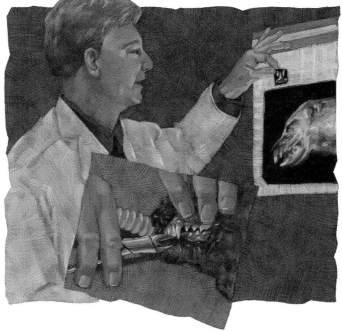

written by Susan Ring
illustrated by Tammy Kutsuma Irvine

SCHOLASTIC INC.
New York Toronto London Auckland Sydney
Mexico City New Delhi Hong Kong Buenos Aires

Developed by Kirchoff/Wohlberg, Inc., in cooperation with Scholastic Inc.

When you need someone to care for your teeth you visit a dentist. When animals need help with their teeth, they can visit a dentist, too! Dr. Carma is a vet who is also a dentist. He takes care of animal teeth.

So far, it is a busy day at Wade Animal Hospital. Dr. Carma is getting a visit from Bucky. He is a small, fluffy, four-year-old dog. It looks like Bucky's gums are very red. He needs to have his teeth cleaned. First, Dr. Carma takes a good look in Bucky's mouth, at his teeth and gums.

Bucky gets a shot that will make him sleepy. Once he is quiet and still, Dr. Carma can look slowly and carefully all around his mouth.

Dr. Carma is ready to clean Bucky's teeth. He uses the same tools that a dentist might use on you. He scrapes Bucky's teeth. He uses a tool called a scaler. This helps break up germs that have built up on Bucky's teeth. He wipes Bucky's mouth with gauze to soak up the blood.

Now Dr. Carma is ready to probe around his mouth. He looks for any teeth that are loose. He finds one. He marks it on the chart.

Dr. Carma takes an x-ray of Bucky's tooth. This will let him know if he can save the tooth. What does the x-ray show? The x-ray shows that the bone is badly worn. The root of the tooth is hardly there. Dr. Carma knows that a bad tooth can be painful for Bucky. That tooth must come out.

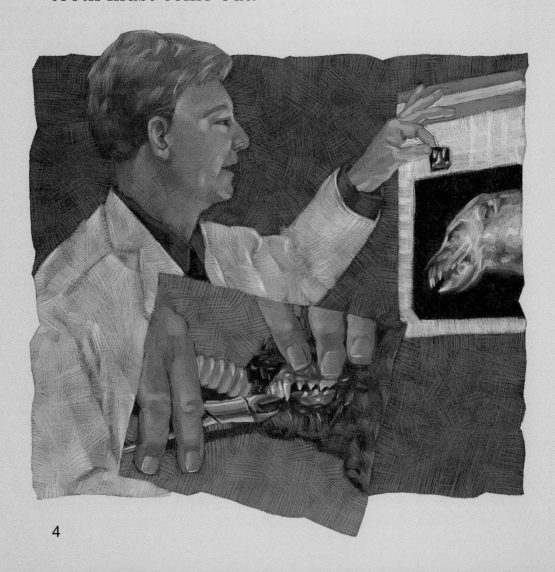

Dr. Carma takes the extractor. It is a tool that he uses to pull out, or extract, the tooth. It comes out easily because it was so loose. Again, he wipes Bucky's mouth with gauze. Bucky is ready to wake up.

"How is Bucky?" asks his owner. "I hope he didn't have any cavities," she adds.

"Dogs don't get cavities!" answers Dr. Carma. "Most of their problems are with bad gums. It is a good thing you brought Bucky in today. Animals who get good dental care live happier and healthier lives."

Dr. Carma hears a squeak. He turns around. "And who is this?" he asks.

"This is Dearie," says the nurse.

Dearie is a two-year-old guinea pig. She has not been eating and seems very unhappy.

"I hope I can help her," says Dr. Carma.

Dr. Carma opens Dearie's tiny mouth. He sees the problem right away.

Dearie's back teeth have grown inward. They have grown so much that they meet in the middle. They have grown over her little tongue. It hurts her.

Dearie squeaks as if to say, "Help me!"

Guinea pigs get tooth problems that are different from those that cats and dogs get. Cats and dogs lose their baby teeth, just the way kids do. Once their adult teeth grow in, the teeth stop growing.

But guinea pigs have teeth that keep growing and growing. Sometimes they keep growing in the wrong direction.

"No wonder Dearie can't eat," says Dr. Carma. "I'm glad you brought her in today."

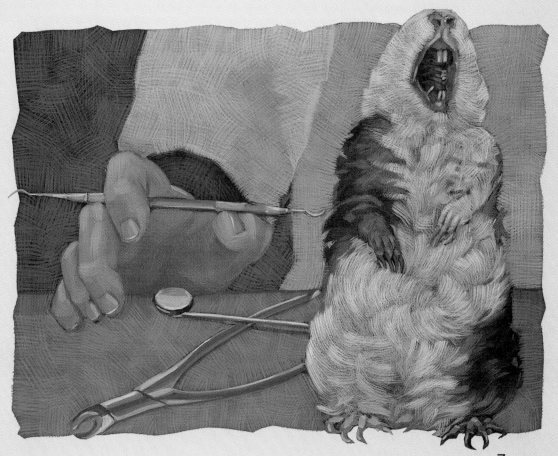

Just as he begins to extract Dearie's teeth, the nurse rushes in. "You have a phone call," she says. "It's an emergency."

"My cat fell off a ledge," cries the girl on the phone. "He broke some teeth."

"Bring him in right away," says Dr. Carma. He walks back to the table and works some more on Dearie. It takes some time. Bucky's worn teeth came out easily. But Dearie's healthy teeth are harder to pull out.

Finally they are out! Dearie will wake up soon and be much happier.

"Your next patient is here," says the
nurse. In comes a girl with a large white cat.

"Fluff is the cat that fell," the nurse says.
Fluff had just come from the orthopedist. That
is a doctor who takes care of bones. The cat
has his leg in a cast.

Wade Animal Hospital has an orthopedist
just for animals. He put Fluff's leg in a cast
because Fluff broke it in the fall. Now it is
time for Dr. Carma to look at Fluff's teeth. Poor
Fluff! He broke two teeth.

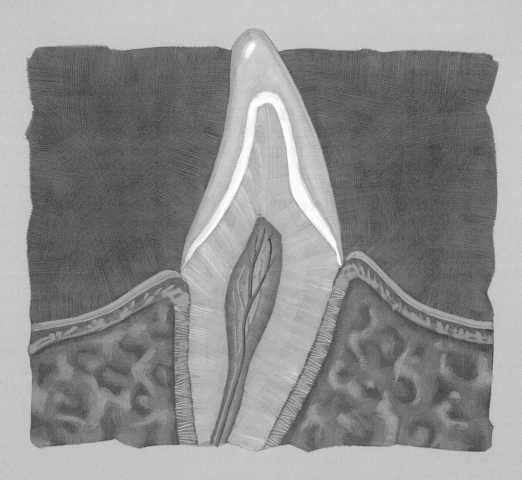

"I am happy to say that his teeth will be okay," says Dr. Carma. "He broke them only a little bit. I can see that the dentine and the nerves look good," he adds.

The dentine is inside the tooth. It is just under the hard outside coating. The nerves run up and down the tooth.

"Fluff will be fine," says the doctor. "He is lucky that all he broke were his leg and two of his teeth."

"Dr. Carma, there's another emergency," says the nurse. "It's the zoo."

Dr. Carma takes the phone. The call is from the vet at the zoo.

"One of our snow leopards has broken a tooth on a fence," says the zoo vet. "One of his keepers saw it this morning when they went in to feed him. He won't eat and he is holding his head in a strange way. I can tell that he is in pain. We know you are busy, but please come right away."

Dr. Carma knows that if he hurries, he might be able to save the tooth. If he gets there too late, the tooth will have to be pulled.

Dr. Carma takes his coat. He packs his bag with as many tools as he can. His helper stays behind. She can take care of the last few visitors that day. Dr. Carma hurries. Once he gets to the sidewalk, he looks for a taxi. He is lucky that one comes quickly.

"To the zoo," he says. "Please take the fastest way."

Dr. Carma gets on his cell phone. "I'm on my way there," he tells the zoo vet. "Please get the snow leopard ready. I should be there in about twenty minutes."

Quite a few vets and zookeepers are waiting for Dr. Carma. They are happy to see him arrive. "We are ready to dart the leopard," the zoo vet says.

Dr. Carma knows that he cannot get close to the snow leopard yet. The zoo vet takes a blow dart. It is a long tube. He puffs air into the tube. Then the dart flies out. It hits the snow leopard very softly.

The snow leopard gets very sleepy. It takes four people to lift the large cat. They put him in the back area. Now Dr. Carma can take a closer look.

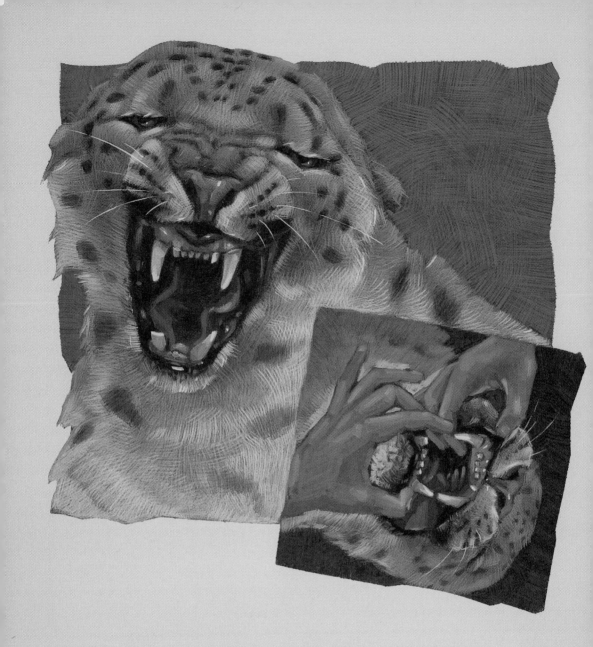

The zoo vet gives the snow leopard something that makes him even more sleepy.

"Okay," says Dr. Carma. "Time to take a look. "I see that this fang fell off very close to the gum line. I'm sorry that I can't save the tooth. I have to pull it out."

"Can he eat without that tooth?" the snow leopard's keeper asks.

"These animals use their big fangs to grab on to their food," Dr. Carma answers. "Now, though, it is more important that the snow leopard is not in pain. Here it comes," Dr. Carma says as he pulls out the tooth.

It is getting late. Dr. Carma is now ready to go home. A man carrying a portable phone stops him. "Dr. Carma, this call is for you. It's from someone at the mounted police stable. He sounds serious."

Dr. Carma listens to the worried police officer. "Can you come and look at my horse's front teeth? We had a spill during training. Something's wrong. I can see blood in the horse's mouth."

"I'll be right there," Dr. Carma answers.